The Monster in My Room

Written by Joy Shepherd

Illustrated by Karalee Hammes

DEDICATION

With Love to my husband Ralph and our three perfect children; Corey, Ryan and Liza.
Having spent many years helping children and families,
I wrote this book to inspire those who are afraid to tell their story.
I am the voice for those who have not yet found their own.

NOTE TO PARENTS
Marion Soloway M.S.W. R.S.W.

This beautifully written and illustrated story for children gets right to the point.
Inappropriate touching should never be a secret.
Using a child's voice, the story takes us through the emotions of a child who has a secret; sadness, fear, anger, empowerment, and resolution.
"When somebody hurts you, you have to tell."
The Monster In My Room is a wonderful tool for parents and educators to help children understand and deal with the idea and reality of inappropriate touching,
which affects "*one in four children...by the time they reach 18.*"

He touched me, he hurt me,
I wanted to yell!

He told me, he told me,
YOU cannot tell!!
"If you tell, I will hurt you
and find you again."
"I know who you are,
I know your name."

He was a bully, this monster is bad.
He touched me, he hurt me,
he made me feel sad.

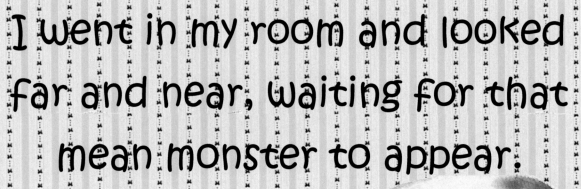

I went in my room and looked far and near, waiting for that mean monster to appear.

I looked under my bed,

opened the drawer,

...and crawled behind the closet door.

I looked out the window,
he knows my name.
If I tell, he will hurt me again!

I climbed into bed,
tired and scared.
What should I do??

The next day at school,
I sat in my chair.

I looked under the bookshelf,

I looked everywhere.

I finished my work
and went out to play.
I wanted to tell,
this monster can't stay.

So scared inside,
I ran up the slide,
went for a ride,
wanting to hide!

The school bell rang,
I heard my name.
My mom is taking me
to my baseball game.

I stood on home plate and
tried not to cry,

if this monster is here,
I will hold my bat high,...
and kick his butt
way up to the sky.

I hit the ball way past the sun.

I ran to the bases

and made a home run.

I smiled, I laughed, I felt so strong!

I have to tell...
something feels wrong!

That night in my room,
my mom held me tight.
I told her what happened
on that terrible night.
"It's not your fault,"
she began to say,
"I'll always love you...
it's going to be ok."

When somebody hurts you, you have to TELL!!!!

YOU SCREAM!!

YOU SHOUT!

Tell your teacher, a parent,
an adult you trust.
You have to tell!
You must! You must!

I stood at the window and
looked up at the sky.
Goodbye bad monster
… goodbye… goodbye!!

ACKNOWLEDGMENTS

Sue-Ellen Welfonder
Thank you for inspiring me to bring pen to paper.

Dr. Roz Doctorow
EdD (Dr. of Education) - Thank you for your friendship and invaluable editorial advice in bringing this book to life.

Marion Soloway M.S.W. R.S.W. (Therapist)
Thank you for understanding me. You are truly the heroine in my story.

Karalee Hammes - Illustrator
Thank you for your wonderful talents, hours of patience...always with a smile.

Made in the USA
Columbia, SC
30 June 2017